The Educator Burnout Recovery Toolkit

Quick strategies to reset your energy, protect your peace, and stay connected to your purpose

Zachary Robbins

Zhazoe Press, LLC

Dedication

For every educator who gives more than anyone sees, this book is dedicated to your resilience, your presence, and your care.

Zhazoe Press Trade eBook Edition, August 2025

Copyright © 2025 Zachary Scott Robbins

All rights reserved.

Zhazoe Press values and supports copyright. Thank you for buying an authorized edition of this book and for complying with copyright laws. No part of this publication may be reproduced, stored in a retrieval system, or transmitted in any form or by any means– electronic, mechanical, photocopying, recording, or otherwise– without the prior written permission of the publisher, except for brief quotations used in reviews or scholarly works.

Published by Zhazoe Publishing

First edition: August 2025

ISBN: 979-8-9997839-2-9

Printed in the United States of America

Disclaimer: This publication is intended for informational and educational purposes only. It does not constitute legal, psychological, or medical advice. The strategies provided are based on research and practical experience, but individual outcomes may vary. The author and publisher disclaim liability for any outcomes resulting from the use or misuse of this material.

Table of Contents

Welcome _____ i

    What You'll Find Inside:
    This guide helps address:
    Each chapter in this guide follows the same structure:

What Burnout Really Looks Like _____ 1

    Burnout Is Not Your Fault: Cognitive and
    Neurological Insights
    WHAT HAPPENED: The Science in Action
    HOW REGULATION COULD HAVE HELPED
    DEBRIEF: What This Teaches Us

Reset in Five Minutes: Simple Yet Effective Strategies to Reset Your Nervous System _____ 10

    Restoring Your Nervous System: Cognitive and
    Neurological Insight
    WHAT HAPPENED: The Science in Action
    HOW REGULATION COULD HAVE
    HELPED EVEN MORE
    DEBRIEF: What This Teaches Us

The Invisible Weight of Teaching _____ 18

    When the Demands of Teaching Feel Too High:
    Cognitive and Neurological Insight
    WHAT HAPPENED: The Science in Action
    HOW REGULATION COULD HAVE HELPED
    DEBRIEF: What This Teaches Us

Teaching Without Losing Yourself: Energy Checks & Recovery Prompts _____ 26

    The Benefits of Pausing and Reflection: Cognitive + Neurological Insight
    WHAT HAPPENED: The Science in Action
    HOW REGULATION COULD HAVE HELPED
    DEBRIEF: What This Teaches Us

Reconnection: Your Impact in Focus _____ 35

    The Benefits of Reconnection: Cognitive + Neurological Insight
    WHAT HAPPENED: The Science in Action
    HOW RECONNECTION COULD HAVE HELPED
    DEBRIEF: What This Teaches Us

From Survival to Renewal: Restoring Meaning and Joy in Your Work _____ 44

    The Science of Joy: Cognitive + Neurological Insight
    WHAT HAPPENED: The Science in Action
    HOW JOY COULD HAVE BEEN REKINDLED
    DEBRIEF: What This Teaches Us

When You're Holding the Team Together _____ 52

    The Cost of Being the Strong One: Cognitive + Neurological Insight
    WHAT HAPPENED: The Science in Action
    HOW REGULATION COULD HAVE HELPED
    DEBRIEF: What This Teaches Us

When Boundaries Feel Impossible _____ 60

    How Setting Boundaries Heals Your Nervous System: Cognitive + Neurological Insight
    WHAT HAPPENED: The Science in Action
    HOW REGULATION COULD HAVE HELPED
    DEBRIEF: What This Teaches Us

When You Feel Like You're Failing Everyone _____ 68

   You're Not Actually Failing: Cognitive + Neurological Insight
   WHAT HAPPENED: The Science in Action
   HOW REGULATION COULD HAVE HELPED
   DEBRIEF: What This Teaches Us

When You're Not Sure You Can Keep Doing This _____ 77

   Why Your Body Freezes, And How to Get Out of it: Cognitive + Neurological Insight
   WHAT HAPPENED: The Science in Action
   HOW REGULATION COULD HAVE HELPED
   DEBRIEF: What This Teaches Us

What to Do Next _____ 84

Want to Go Deeper? _____ 85

References and Further Reading _____ 86

About the Author _____ 90

Welcome

Teaching is purpose-driven work. It can be intellectually engaging and deeply meaningful–but also emotionally taxing and physically exhausting in ways noneducators will never fully understand. You are managing emotions, redirecting behaviors, juggling expectations, responding to interruptions, and adapting constantly. Often, you do all of this with very little time to catch your breath, let alone reflect, recharge, or feel a sense of accomplishment before the next wave of student needs, administrative demands, or unexpected disruptions demands your attention.

The mental load on teachers is relentless. Staying present and responsive to every student's needs can wear you down well before the end of the workday.

This toolkit is designed for practicing educators who live that reality every day. It is not built around theory or generic advice. It offers strategies that work in real classrooms, with real students, under real constraints. These are tools you can use during the day, during transitions, while teaching, or even while talking with a student.

The Educator Burnout Recovery Toolkit

You do not need to leave your classroom to feel more regulated. You don't need to wait for a break or a workshop to take care of yourself. Everything in this guide is designed to support your well-being while you are still at work.

Your well-being matters just as much as your teaching performance. You deserve practical, research-informed strategies that help you hold onto your clarity and calm, even when the demands keep piling up.

What You'll Find Inside:

- Evidence-based micro-strategies
- Reflective prompts
- Wellness practices grounded in neuroscience and trauma-informed care
- Support for real challenges like emotional exhaustion, boundary setting, and impostor syndrome

This guide helps address:

- Emotional exhaustion and compassion fatigue
- Chronic stress and nervous system overload
- Guilt from setting boundaries
- Disconnect from purpose
- Team dysfunction or lack of support

The Educator Burnout Recovery Toolkit

Each chapter in this guide follows the same structure:

- An introduction to an aspect of burnout
- Cognitive and neurological insights that break down an element of burnout
- A case scenario of how a teacher experiences a facet of burnout
- A breakdown of the science in action, and how it impacts teachers physically, mentally, and emotionally
- How regulation could have helped in the case scenario
- Takeaways from the case study and chapter
- Try This! – tips to restore calm

"You don't have to fix everything today. You just need a way to begin again."

What Burnout Really Looks Like

Burnout is not just about being tired; it's about feeling deeply exhausted and emotionally depleted. Tiredness can be solved with rest, a weekend of sleep, or a few days away from work. Burnout runs deeper. Burnout is the slow, silent erosion of your capacity to care, to focus, and to feel like yourself in the classroom. This kind of depletion happens when the emotional labor of teaching demands more than your nervous system can sustain, day after day. Burnout isn't a sudden crash; it's a gradual unraveling. It is a steady leak, a quiet unraveling that becomes impossible to ignore.

You may still be meeting expectations by consistently lesson planning, calling parents, managing behaviors, and attending meetings. You might still smile at your students. However, if you are burned out, all of that begins to happen with a quiet, empty feeling inside. You feel less connected to your students and less motivated by your work. You may begin to question your impact. Some reach a point where they stop feeling much of anything at all.

What you're experiencing isn't a failure of effort or resilience. It is your body's way of protecting you from chronic overload. When your emotional resources are constantly depleted by managing students, navigating staff dynamics, and meeting administrative demands, without space to recover or time to focus on your own needs, your nervous system begins to shut down non-essential functions. When this happens, your body begins to pull energy away from empathy, curiosity, and joy. Your brain shifts into survival mode, focused just on getting through the day.

This survival mode is what many teachers refer to as "robot mode." You move through the motions of your school day on autopilot. You do what's expected, but it costs more than anyone can see. Even the parts of the job that once brought you joy, such as laughing with students, collaborating with a colleague, and leading a rich discussion, start to feel hollow. Emotionally, you begin to shut down. You still care, but it feels distant.

You might feel guilty for not doing more. You might compare yourself to colleagues who seem unaffected. You might keep pushing, believing that stopping means failure. But the longer you ignore what your nervous system is telling you, the more burnout seeps into your body. Your sleep becomes shallow. Your mind struggles with even small decisions. Minor irritations feel magnified. Even extended breaks stop feeling restorative.

Burnout is not a personal shortcoming. It is not a lack of love for your students or a sign that you are not cut out for this work. It is a physiological and emotional response to chronic conditions that demand more than your body and mind were built to carry alone.

Burnout Is Not Your Fault: Cognitive and Neurological Insights

A 2022 survey by Rand found that teachers experience stress at more than double the rate of other working adults. K–12 educators report the highest levels of burnout of any profession in the United States (Steiner et al., 2022).

Nearly half of all K–12 teachers say they feel burned out often or always. Over half say they plan to leave the profession earlier than they originally intended (Marken & Agrawal, 2022). In 2021, almost one in three teachers were chronically absent (Jones et al., 2021). If you're reading this, there's a good chance you're reflected in those numbers.

Burnout is not a personal failure. According to the National Education Association, burnout happens when an educator has exhausted the personal and professional resources needed to do the job (Walker, 2021). Maslach and Leiter describe it through three dimensions: emotional exhaustion, depersonalization, and reduced personal accomplishment (Maslach & Leiter, 2016). Each of these has roots in the nervous system and creates specific impacts on your thinking, feelings, and behavior.

Emotional exhaustion is not just about being tired. It's the depletion of emotional and mental energy. In this state, you may struggle to solve problems, manage your emotions, or stay connected to others. Your nervous system becomes less able to handle stress and more likely to shut down, withdraw, or overreact.

Depersonalization shows up as emotional distance. You might begin to view students, colleagues, or even yourself with detachment

The Educator Burnout Recovery Toolkit

when the demands on your energy have been high for too long. This distancing is not a sign of apathy or lack of care. It's the brain protecting itself from overload by creating space where it can.

Reduced personal accomplishment is the sense that your work no longer makes a difference. You may feel ineffective or unseen, even when you're trying your hardest. This weakens motivation, erodes self-confidence, and often leads to self-blame.

Each of these reactions reveals the strain of chronic stress on the brain. When your nervous system is overwhelmed, your limbic system, the part of the brain that processes emotion, stays activated and constantly scans for threats or mistakes (Porges, 2011). This creates a baseline of anxiety and reactivity. Meanwhile, the prefrontal cortex, your center for focus, memory, empathy, and decision-making, becomes less active.

You may notice it when you forget things more often, struggle to concentrate, or lose your temper more easily. What used to feel manageable now feels like too much. These are not changes in your character. They are signs that your brain and body are under strain.

The good news is that burnout is reversible. But recovery requires more than time off. It calls for intentional practices that support your nervous system, reduce chronic stress signals, and restore access to the parts of your brain that support calm, connection, and clarity.

Small actions like slow breathing, grounding movement, reflection, and setting boundaries can help. Talking with trusted colleagues can also provide relief, perspective, and a sense that you're not alone. But perhaps the most important first step is letting go of the belief that burnout means you failed. It doesn't. Burnout is your body's way of telling you something needs to change. It's asking for rest, repair, and a return to safety.

CASE SCENARIO:
"Mr. Navarro Can't Feel Anything Anymore"

It was a Wednesday morning in March. Mr. Navarro sat in his car in the school parking lot, staring at the building. He wasn't crying. He wasn't panicking. He just felt blank. He had no energy, no dread, and no motivation. He felt nothingness and emptiness.

He wasn't new to teaching. He'd been teaching sixth grade for over a decade. He had routines, systems, even backup lesson plans. He knew how to manage a classroom. He knew how to teach. But lately, something had changed.

The day before, his student, Amari, had quietly drawn a picture of a broken heart and left it on her desk. Mr. Navarro noticed it after class and tucked it into his binder to check in with her later. But he never did. He didn't even feel guilty about it. He just forgot.

That scared him.

That morning, as he finally stepped out of the car, his legs felt heavy. He walked to his room like someone walking into a job they no longer recognized. His students were already waiting. One of them was tapping a pencil on the desk. Another kept calling out, "Mr. Navarro! Mr. Navarro!" He didn't answer right away. His mind couldn't focus enough to respond.

He started class, but everything felt off. His words came out flat. He couldn't remember the transitions between activities. When two students began whispering and laughing in the corner, he just stared at them. He knew he should redirect them, but he didn't care enough to make the effort. He wasn't angry. He wasn't sad. He was just... gone.

When the final bell rang that day, Mr. Navarro didn't pack up. He just sat at his desk. The building emptied. The lights dimmed. He finally picked up his phone and typed out a message to a colleague:

"I think something's wrong. I can't feel anything anymore."

WHAT HAPPENED: The Science in Action

Mr. Navarro was not simply tired. He was experiencing classic symptoms of burnout. His nervous system, after years of prolonged stress without enough recovery, had shifted into protective shutdown mode. His body was conserving energy by shutting down emotional engagement. This is the root of what Maslach and Leiter refer to as emotional exhaustion and depersonalization (Maslach & Leiter, 2016).

Instead of reacting to stress with panic or outbursts, Mr. Navaro's system had gone quiet. In neurological terms, his limbic system, which manages emotional processing, had been overactivated for too long. In response, his brain deprioritized emotional sensitivity to conserve energy. The prefrontal cortex, responsible for executive function, empathy, and decision-making, had limited access. That's why he forgot to check in with Amari. That's why he couldn't respond when his students called out to him. His brain was no longer functioning from a regulated, connected place. It was operating from depletion.

The emotional numbness he was experiencing wasn't about weakness or lack of effort. It was his body's way of adapting to constant stress in an environment that offered little space to recover or feel emotionally safe.

HOW REGULATION COULD HAVE HELPED

Mr. Navarro didn't need a vacation. He needed a nervous system reset.

If he had paused weeks earlier when he first noticed that teaching no longer felt meaningful and he felt himself going numb, he might have caught the signs of emotional exhaustion before they deepened. A regular two-minute morning check-in, such as "How do I feel today? What's one thing I need?" could have helped him monitor his internal state before it reached crisis levels.

Mr. Navarro also needed support in return. He needed someone to notice the weight he was carrying and check in on him. If he had access to a safe space to talk through his stress, he might have been able to interrupt the shutdown response before it took hold. Feeling seen, heard, and supported might have reengaged the parts of Mr. Navarro's brain responsible for motivation, memory, and emotional regulation.

Even brief moments, such as reflecting on a meaningful interaction or receiving a kind word, could have activated dopamine and oxytocin, helping restore his motivation, emotional balance, and sense of connection.

DEBRIEF: What This Teaches Us

What Mr. Navarro endured was burnout. Burnout is not always loud. It doesn't always come with tears or anger. Sometimes it's silent. Sometimes it looks like doing the job, meeting expectations, and checking all the workplace boxes while your internal world is going dark.

Burnout often masquerades as detachment or apathy, but it is your nervous system's way of saying: I've been running on empty for too long. I can't keep pretending this is sustainable.

Mr. Navarro didn't experience a lack of care. His burnout and resulting fatigue were the result of caring deeply, for too long, without enough support or recovery. His body began to shut down access to the very qualities that once made him effective — empathy, patience, and presence.

The key takeaway from Mr. Navarro's story is this: you don't have to wait until you feel numb to make a change. Pay attention to the early signs: heaviness, emotional distance, and a lack of joy. These are not flaws. They are signals that can be addressed.

Healing from burnout doesn't require perfection. The process begins by noticing, naming, and normalizing your stress response, then taking small, science-backed steps to give your nervous system the safety it needs to recover.

TRY THIS:

- Name what you're carrying: Say out loud, "I'm holding too much today, and it's okay to feel that."
- Use a reset phrase: Pick one line that grounds you. Example: "This is hard. And I'm doing my best."
- Stand tall, breathe deep: Put both feet flat on the floor. Inhale for 4, exhale for 6. Repeat 3 times.
- Talk it through: Choose a trusted colleague to debrief with after a draining day.
- Release one pressure: Pick one unrealistic expectation to let go of, just for today.

Reset in Five Minutes: Simple Yet Effective Strategies to Reset Your Nervous System

You might not have time to take a walk around the block to reset emotionally. You might not have a quiet space to meditate. You may not even have the luxury of an uninterrupted prep period. But none of this means you cannot reset.

In a school day packed with back-to-back responsibilities, resetting your nervous system may seem impossible. You are constantly thinking ahead, managing the energy of your classroom, responding to emails, redirecting behaviors, and trying to remember what you were doing before the last interruption pulled you off course. The idea of rest can feel out of reach. However, neuroscience suggests that meaningful regulation does not require an hour. It doesn't even require ten minutes (Bentley et al., 2023).

You can reset your stress response in five minutes or less. What matters is not the length of time but the intention behind it. Short, deliberate practices can shift your nervous system out of activation and into recovery. These brief resets are not just feel-good moments. They are evidence-based interventions that help your brain function more clearly and your body respond more effectively, even while the demands of the day continue around you.

A five-minute reset might look like stepping into the hallway and taking ten deep, steady breaths while focusing on the rise and fall of your chest. It might be placing a hand on your heart and repeating a grounding phrase like "I am here. I am safe. I can slow down" (*Grounding Strategies to Calm Your Nervous System*, n.d.). It might mean humming quietly to yourself while resetting the room between classes, or walking slowly to the copier while staying connected to your breath and body. These simple acts are more than coping tools. They are biological cues that tell your brain you are not under threat, and you can recover right here in the middle of your workday.

When practiced consistently, these small resets begin to retrain your nervous system. Instead of staying stuck in tension or overstimulation, your body gradually learns how to return more quickly to a state of calm, focus, and emotional balance. That shift makes a significant difference in how you interact with students. It affects your tone in emails. It changes how you respond to disruptions, challenges, or urgencies.

You don't have to wait until you reach your breaking point to make a change. You don't need to hold out for the weekend to feel relief. You can build a habit of slowing down and resetting your nervous system in small, sustainable ways, starting with just five minutes at a time.

Restoring Your Nervous System: Cognitive and Neurological Insight

In the previous section, we explored how burnout changes the brain. Emotional exhaustion, detachment, and reduced motivation are not simply psychological states. They are signs of a nervous system that has been overactivated and a prefrontal cortex that has been overwhelmed. This section explores how short, intentional practices can begin to reverse those effects.

The nervous system constantly scans the environment for cues of safety or threat. When it detects stress, whether from a classroom interaction, workload pressure, or emotional strain, it activates the sympathetic nervous system (Porges, 2011). This fight-or-flight response increases heart rate, tightens muscles, limits digestion, narrows your attention, and directs energy away from the prefrontal cortex. In this mode, it becomes difficult to think clearly, access empathy, or make reasoned decisions (Maslach & Leiter, 2016).

Physical and emotional recovery requires the activation of the parasympathetic nervous system. More specifically, it depends on the vagus nerve, which plays a key role in calming the body after stress. When the vagus nerve is activated, it signals the body to slow down. Breathing deepens, heart rate slows, and the mind begins to clear. This activation helps the body exit survival mode and allows cognitive resources to return (Bentley et al., 2023).

What helps activate the vagus nerve are slow, rhythmic, sensory-based practices such as breathing exercises, mindful movement, humming, chanting, grounding through physical touch, and guided visualization. Each of these practices can be done in five minutes and provides a clear signal to your nervous system that it is safe to release tension (Bentley et al., 2023).

Over time, these short resets lead to lasting change. This process is known as neuroplasticity, the brain's ability to reorganize itself based on experience (Thayer et al., 2012). When calming practices are used regularly, the nervous system becomes more responsive to safety cues and quicker to recover from stress (Brown, 2009).

These five-minute practices are not luxuries. They are essential tools for sustaining your well-being. They counteract the neurological patterns that burnout creates and support your ability to stay regulated, present, and clear-headed in challenging environments.

This is not about avoiding the real demands of teaching. It is about creating internal conditions that allow you to meet those demands without breaking down. For educators experiencing constant pressure, these resets offer one of the most reliable and sustainable ways to care for both the brain and the body.

TRY THIS:

- Box breathing: Inhale for 4, hold for 4, exhale for 4, hold for 4. Repeat four rounds.
- Visual grounding: Find one thing in the room and describe it with five details.
- Tension scan: Clench fists and jaw. Then release slowly and completely.

The Educator Burnout Recovery Toolkit

- Name your emotion: Say: "I'm feeling ___ right now, and that's valid."
- Text a small win: Tell a teammate one thing that went right today.

CASE SCENARIO:
"Ms. Bennett's Copier Reset"

It was second period, and Ms. Bennett already felt like she was drowning. The morning started with a late bus, three parent emails, and a student meltdown in homeroom. Her coffee had gone cold. Her shoulders were tight. And her co-teacher had just texted to say they'd be out sick... again.

She was trying to stay composed, but everything grated on her nerves: a student chewing bubble gum too loudly; another tapping a pencil without realizing it. Her voice felt sharp, even when she didn't mean it to be. At one point, she gave a direction, then instantly forgot what she said. She could hear herself rushing through her lesson, and it only made her more irritated.

By the time the bell rang, she felt wired and tired at the same time.

She picked up her folder and headed toward the copier room with a stack of handouts. Halfway there, she caught her reflection in a window. She looked tense, edgy, and not herself. She paused.

Instead of rushing into battle with the copier, she leaned against the wall and closed her eyes.

She took a long, slow inhale, counting to four, and then exhaled for six. One hand rested lightly over her heart. She whispered to herself:

"You're okay. You're safe. You can slow down."

She repeated the breath three more times.

Then she opened her eyes, picked up the folder, and walked into the copier room, slower this time. She felt her shoulders drop just a little. Her face softened. When she returned to her classroom, she greeted the next group of students with more ease. She hadn't solved every problem, but she had interrupted the spiral of stress and self-doubt. And that changed everything.

WHAT HAPPENED: The Science in Action

Ms. Bennett experienced a low-level but cumulative stress buildup, something many educators experience without realizing it. Her nervous system had been operating in sympathetic activation for hours: fast pace, shallow breath, racing thoughts, tight muscles. This state narrows perception and disrupts the brain's ability to access empathy and memory, exactly the capacities teachers rely on most.

By pausing in the hallway and intentionally breathing with a longer exhale, she activated her vagus nerve, the main driver of the parasympathetic nervous system, which helps bring the body out of the fight-or-flight response. Her hand over her heart added physical grounding, which sent a secondary cue of safety to her brain. Her whispered affirmation anchored the experience with language, reinforcing emotional regulation.

These small, layered actions engaged the biological mechanisms responsible for downshifting stress, even in the middle of a busy school day.

HOW REGULATION COULD HAVE HELPED EVEN MORE

Ms. Bennett did something powerful: she recognized the signs of dysregulation early and took action. However, this reset didn't have to be a one-time event. If she made it a daily practice, five minutes between classes or before lunch, her nervous system would begin to adapt.

Regular use of sensory-based interventions, such as breathwork, grounding touch, and affirmations, fosters neuroplasticity, which is the brain's capacity to rewire itself for faster recovery and greater resilience.

Even something as simple as humming softly, stretching slowly, or walking to the copier with deliberate attention to her breath can serve as a mini reset. These subtle shifts help maintain emotional bandwidth and prevent stress from escalating into overwhelming feelings.

DEBRIEF: What This Teaches Us

Regulation doesn't always look like yoga or silence. Sometimes it looks like a hallway pause, a hand on your chest, or a quiet breath when no one's watching. These small resets aren't indulgent, they're strategic and imperative.

Ms. Bennett didn't have a break, a quiet room, or even a moment of true privacy. However, she had five minutes. She used those minutes with intention.

This is the key: you don't need ideal conditions to reclaim calm. You only need awareness, a simple practice, and a willingness to start.

Educators are taught to push through challenging moments, but resilience isn't just about enduring stress; it's also about cultivating a positive mindset. Five minutes of deep breathing, movement, or quiet reflection can interrupt the cycle. Five minutes of intentional care can help you reset and feel more like yourself again. Over time, those five minutes become a nervous system blueprint for staying grounded, no matter what the day throws at you.

The Invisible Weight of Teaching

Your responsibilities as a teacher are often framed as necessary, urgent, and non-negotiable. You are expected to differentiate instruction for every learner, regardless of ability. You're tasked with building strong relationships with every student, while also contacting families, addressing behavioral issues, planning for IEP accommodations, managing transitions, and entering data into multiple platforms by the end of the week. You're asked to give up prep time for meetings and stay emotionally available for every crisis that walks through your door.

Even when you care deeply about your students, the pressure can feel relentless. Some mornings, you wake up already feeling behind. Your to-do list is longer than the hours in your day, and the stakes feel too high to let anything slip. Guilt sets in quickly. You wonder if you're doing enough. You question whether anyone truly sees the weight of your workload or the effort it takes to keep going. And somewhere along the way, you start to believe the lie. You start to believe that feeling overwhelmed is a personal failure, rather than what it really is: a sign of a system stretched too thin and stretching you too thin.

What makes it even harder is that much of your emotional load goes unseen. To your colleagues, you may appear calm, composed, and even get praised for your professionalism. But beneath the surface, the strain is real, and it takes a toll. You work through lunch. You answer messages long after the day should be over. You keep pushing past your limits because slowing down feels like letting someone down. And over time, that quiet stretching of yourself creates an emotional exhaustion no checklist can fix.

You are not the problem. The problem is the numerous expectations placed on you. This pressure is not a sign of weakness. It is a reflection of a system that was never designed with sustainability in mind. What you're feeling isn't personal failure. It's what happens when a deeply meaningful job is overloaded with demands and emotional labor no one person should have to carry alone or can sustain.

When the Demands of Teaching Feel Too High: Cognitive and Neurological Insight

In earlier sections, we explored how chronic stress impairs emotional regulation and cognitive clarity. Here, we go deeper into how the brain responds when the demands of teaching feel unrelenting.

The human brain is wired to prioritize threat detection (Imad, 2022). In environments filled with urgency and unpredictability, like schools, the nervous system becomes reactive, not only to actual emergencies but to anything that feels pressing. This pattern favors urgency over importance, leading the brain to misfire stress responses even when no real danger is present (Victor et al., 2024).

This shift toward short-term survival is driven by two core systems in the brain: the limbic system, which is responsible for emotional reactivity, and the prefrontal cortex, which supports planning, organization, and thoughtful decision-making. Under chronic stress, the limbic system stays dominant. It scans for emotional pressure and keeps your body in a state of vigilance. At the same time, the prefrontal cortex, the part of the brain you rely on to stay grounded, reflective, and intentional, becomes harder to access (Girotti et al., 2017; Reising, 2013).

When this imbalance between threat detection and higher-order thinking takes hold, your work becomes reactive. You may start many tasks, but struggle to complete them. You may agree to new responsibilities even when your schedule is full. You may feel pulled to act quickly without stepping back to assess your true priorities. This is not a failure of willpower. It is your brain responding to sustained overload by favoring speed over clarity and output over strategy (Imad, 2022).

The way out of this cycle is not to push through. It is to pause, intentionally and repeatedly. These pauses help reset the nervous system and shift the brain out of reactivity. A minute of slow breathing, stepping away from noise or stimulation, or even writing down one thing that can wait can help re-activate the prefrontal cortex and reduce the sense of internal pressure to keep pushing or performing.

Over time, these moments of reset strengthen your brain's ability to access calm, clarity, and choice. They help your nervous system regain a sense of control, even when external demands remain high (Victor et al., 2024). You begin to move with intention rather than urgency.

The Educator Burnout Recovery Toolkit

Your value is not measured by the number of tasks you complete. It is reflected in your ability to discern what truly matters, to conserve your energy, and to protect the inner steadiness that makes sustained care possible. These small shifts are not signs of slowing down. They are the foundation of sustainable teaching.

TRY THIS:

- Identify invisible labor: Write down three things you do that no one sees. Decide if they still serve your purpose.
- Cancel one thing: Take a look at your to-do list. Cross out one non-essential item.
- Set a "good enough" goal: Choose one area where you'll aim for 80%, not perfection.
- Delay without guilt: Move one task to next week. Say: "It's not urgent, and I need space."
- Write your top 3: Each morning, list your three most important tasks. Let the rest go.

CASE SCENARIO:
"Mr. Delgado's Breaking Point"

It was Tuesday, but it already felt like the end of the week.

Mr. Delgado arrived at school early to catch up on grading, but his inbox had other plans. He had three messages from parents, a last-minute IEP meeting invite, and a flagged reminder to update behavior logs in the district's new system by 3:00 p.m.

The Educator Burnout Recovery Toolkit

By first period, one student was melting down over a missed breakfast. Another refused to come into the room, and two others needed different accommodations for the same assignment. He made it work, as always, but it left him drained.

During his prep period, just as he opened his laptop to revise tomorrow's lesson plan, his principal stepped in.

"Quick favor," she said. "Can you cover Ms. Jenkins' class for 30 minutes? I know you've got a full plate, but you're always so reliable."

He said yes. Of course, he said yes.

By lunchtime, he hadn't eaten. His throat was sore, and his head was spinning from the constant noise of the classroom. Still, he returned two parent calls and logged a behavior referral, afraid he might forget if he waited.

When the final bell rang, he sat at his desk and stared at the to-do list he hadn't touched. His body was heavy. His mind was foggy. He scrolled through the unread messages in his inbox and felt himself mentally crack, not loudly, but quietly.

He didn't cry. He didn't yell. He just sat there, still, with his hands on the keyboard, too exhausted to type, too overwhelmed to think.

WHAT HAPPENED: The Science in Action

Mr. Delgado was facing cognitive overload–pushed there by a relentless stream of unrealistic demands. His nervous system shifted into a chronic state of sympathetic activation, marked by the fight, flight, or freeze response. This physiological shift didn't happen because he lacked resilience. It happened because he felt constant pressure to prove he could handle everything without showing signs of struggle.

Each new demand triggered his limbic system, especially the amygdala, which constantly scanned for threats. His brain couldn't tell the difference between emotional stress and actual danger. It only knew one thing: this is too much, too fast, with no end in sight.

At the same time, his prefrontal cortex, the part of his brain responsible for focus, setting boundaries, and big-picture thinking, started to dim. It became harder for Mr. Delgado to plan. It became harder for him to prioritize, harder to say no, and harder to act on what mattered most. So he said yes to tasks he didn't have capacity for, started projects he couldn't finish, and stared at his to-do list in silence when the rare chance to catch up finally came.

His biology wasn't failing. It was protecting him the only way it knew how—by shifting into survival mode, laser-focused on one thing: just make it through the day.

HOW REGULATION COULD HAVE HELPED

If Mr. Delgado had recognized the signs of nervous system overload earlier, small, intentional interventions could have disrupted the downward spiral of stress, exhaustion, and emotional withdrawal. Just thirty seconds of slow, conscious breathing after agreeing to cover that extra class could have helped re-engage his prefrontal cortex. A simple pause to jot down one clear priority before opening his email might have offered a sense of direction, a moment of grounding before the next wave hit.

Later, he could have paused to ask himself: *What's actually mine to carry today?* That reflection could have helped him delegate a task or postpone a deadline. It could even help him to respond differently the next time his principal steps into his class for another "quick" favor. He could simply say, "I'm at capacity," or add, "but thank you for acknowledging my reliability. I really appreciate it."

These aren't signs of weakness. They're acts of preservation. And each one sends a powerful signal to the brain: that it's safe to slow down now. You don't have to outrun the day to prove you care.

DEBRIEF: What This Teaches Us

What happened to Mr. Delgado isn't rare. It's what unfolds when a system normalizes chronic overextension and calls it professionalism.

Teachers aren't failing at their jobs; they're being overwhelmed by demands that exceed what the human nervous system can sustain. The struggle teachers experience has little to do with competence. The struggle is often a result of outdated expectations that no longer align with the realities of teaching today. The longer this mismatch is ignored, the more teachers begin to internalize the lie that they are the problem.

Mr. Delgado didn't break down because he was weak. He hit a wall because his body had reached its limit. Even the most committed educators have a breaking point.

When teachers are expected to be constantly available, manage intense emotional demands, and take on growing workloads, those expectations can become unmanageable. In that context, regulation is not a luxury; it is a lifeline. It becomes a quiet form of resistance and a way of saying, "I will not sacrifice my clarity, my energy, or my sense of self."

Every time you pause to breathe, to say no, or to reclaim a single moment of stillness, you're not stepping away from the work. You're protecting your capacity to stay in it with presence and purpose. You're protecting your ability to stay grounded in a role that you love, but should not cost you your well-being.

Teaching Without Losing Yourself: Energy Checks & Recovery Prompts

Teaching often feels like a nonstop relay race. From the moment you walk through the school doors, your attention is pulled in many directions. You answer a student's question while keeping an eye on classroom behavior. You troubleshoot a tech issue while mentally adjusting your lesson. You're tracking accommodations, managing shifting dynamics, supporting emotional needs, and trying to fit in planning during brief moments of unclaimed time. Even your prep period is rarely your own. Sometimes during prep periods, you help a colleague, catch up on paperwork, or think about the next block of instruction.

What gets lost in this relentless pace is you.

You stop paying attention to how you actually feel. You push past your exhaustion. You ignore the tightness in your chest, the irritation behind your eyes, or the edge creeping into your tone. You power through until your body forces you to notice.

You snap at a student. You forget something important. You feel a deep weariness that no single night of rest can undo.

In a job like this, reflective check-ins are not a luxury; they are essential. They're a necessity— a form of emotional hygiene. Just as you wouldn't expect a computer to run indefinitely without rebooting, your mind and body need regular opportunities to pause, reset, and process. These check-ins don't need to be long or complicated. They require only a few quiet moments to ask yourself:

- *What am I holding right now?*
- *What's draining me?*
- *What's restoring me?*
- *Where am I carrying this stress in my body?*

By asking these questions regularly, you will begin to recognize patterns. You will start to identify what keeps you grounded, as well as what doesn't. You create an internal awareness that gives you the power to intervene *before* your nervous system tips into exhaustion. These small recovery prompts aren't meant to fix everything in the moment. They help you hold onto your sense of self, even while caring for everyone else.

Recovery happens in small moments, such as in the breath you take between classes, in the moment you step outside after a tense interaction, in the quiet pause where you name the emotion behind your tension. These acts of self-awareness build strength. They're powerful. They restore your clarity. They strengthen your presence.

They help you stay rooted in your values instead of swept up by your exhaustion.

The Benefits of Pausing and Reflection: Cognitive + Neurological Insight

Your brain is constantly filtering noise, tracking movement, reading tone, and interpreting emotion. In the classroom, that stream of input rarely stops. When demands pile up without any pause to process, the nervous system shifts into high alert. The brain starts treating even neutral input as a potential threat (Holland, 2025).

This heightened stress response is driven by the limbic system—especially the amygdala—which is responsible for detecting danger. As pressure builds, the amygdala overactivates. Your heart rate rises. Your breath becomes shallow. Focus narrows. Even in the absence of immediate risk, your body prepares to defend, solve, or fix (Holland, 2025). In this state, connecting with others, managing your reactions, or making thoughtful decisions becomes harder.

Earlier sections in this toolkit explored how this stress activation can hijack attention and shrink access to your prefrontal cortex, the part of your brain responsible for planning, empathy, and problem-solving. The path back begins with reflection (Maslach & Leiter, 2016).

Reflection helps shift control from the emotional brain back to the thinking brain. When you pause to name what you're feeling, notice physical tension, or ask yourself what's needed, the prefrontal cortex re-engages. That doesn't remove the stress, but it reduces its intensity. It restores the mental distance needed to respond instead of react (Maslach & Leiter, 2016).

This simple habit also helps prevent decision fatigue. When you stay disconnected from your inner state, your brain has to work harder to interpret emotions, suppress discomfort, and stay productive. Over time, that hidden labor leads to exhaustion (Holland, 2025). But checking in even briefly eases that mental load. It helps your system stop bracing for what's next and start recovering from what's already happened.

A few minutes of intentional awareness can calm the stress response. This practice communicates safety to your nervous system and makes space for recovery (Porges, 2011). You build emotional stamina not by ignoring your limits but by honoring them.

Sustainable work requires presence, and presence requires care. When you tune in and respond to what your body and mind are telling you, you preserve the clarity, steadiness, and emotional strength that allow you to keep going.

QUICK PROMPTS:

- What part of your day drains you most?
- What brings you relief or joy?
- What are you doing out of guilt?
- Where could you say no more confidently?

The Educator Burnout Recovery Toolkit

TRY THIS:

- Move your body before your mind races: Walk one lap around the school before or after your most stressful class.
- Designate one "white space" block in your schedule each week: no grading or planning, just time for you.
- Use the 3:1 rule: For every three things you do out of obligation, do one thing just for joy.
- Practice a daily closing ritual: When you get home at the end of your day, light a candle, play a calming song, or say aloud, "I did enough today."
- Start your week with an energy map: Color-code your schedule based on what gives you energy versus what drains it. Adjust one thing accordingly.

CASE SCENARIO:
"Ms. Lee Didn't Know She Was Drained"

It was fourth period, and Ms. Lee was halfway through her day. On the surface, everything seemed fine. She had just wrapped up a vocabulary warm-up, redirected a side conversation, and made a quick mental note to check in with a student who seemed off.

But something didn't feel right, and she couldn't quite name it

Her shoulders were tense. Her mouth was dry. She'd read the same sentence three times, but the words blurred together. Nothing was sinking in. Then a student raised her hand. It was a question Ms. Lee normally welcomed—an honest, clarifying *why* about the concept she was teaching.

But instead of answering it, she snapped, "Just follow the directions!"

The student froze. The room went still.

Ms. Lee paused, instantly feeling regret. She hadn't meant to sound harsh. The question was valid. The student hadn't done anything wrong. But in that moment, even a simple question felt overwhelming.

At lunch, she didn't eat. She sat slouched in her chair, scrolling aimlessly through her phone, trying to shake the heaviness she was feeling. When her co-teacher stopped by to ask a question about their afternoon block, she nodded—but didn't hear a word.

She made it through the rest of the day. No major disruptions. No outward signs that anything was wrong. From the outside, she looked like she had it all together.

But when she got into her car, she didn't start it. She sat still, keys in her lap, too tired to move. Her chest ached. Her eyes burned. She couldn't remember the last time she paused to notice how she was really feeling, and now, the weight of everything she hadn't processed came rushing in, all at once.

She hadn't realized how drained she was until there was nothing left to give.

WHAT HAPPENED: The Science in Action

Ms. Lee's nervous system was operating under chronic cognitive load. There was no single crisis. No dramatic moment signaled the shift. Instead, the wear came from countless small stressors that steadily wore her down.

All day, she had been responding to students' emotions, making rapid decisions about lessons and logistics, juggling competing needs, and redirecting classroom behavior. She did it all without pause. Her attention was split, her energy stretched thin, yet she kept going because that's what teachers do.

But without time to pause or reflect, her limbic system remained on high alert, absorbing the endless stream of student needs, split-second decisions, and emotional labor as ongoing threats. And her body responded in kind. This kept her in a low-level sympathetic state, marked by an elevated heart rate, muscle tension, narrowed focus, and reduced emotional tolerance.

Because she hadn't taken a moment to reflect or reset, her prefrontal cortex wasn't fully online. It's the part of the brain that supports regulation, empathy, and reflection. As the day wore on, her tone sharpened. Her focus faltered. Interactions felt strained, not because she didn't care, but because connection had become another task she struggled to sustain.

This wasn't a breakdown. It was dysregulation—the quiet kind that builds slowly over time. The kind that whispers instead of shouts, until eventually, the body demands to be heard.

HOW REGULATION COULD HAVE HELPED

If Ms. Lee had taken even 60 seconds between classes for a brief energy check-in, she might have interrupted the spiral.

A simple internal scan could have made a difference.

- *Where am I feeling tension?*
- *What is my current energy level?*
- *What is one thing I need right now?*

Just one slow breath. One moment of naming what she was feeling—overwhelmed, scattered, on edge. That small act of awareness could have helped re-engage her prefrontal cortex, the part of her brain that can restore her clarity, regulation, and empathy. With that awareness, she could have responded to her student in a calmer, more grounded way.

Even something as simple as walking slowly to the copier while focusing on her breath, or placing a hand on her chest and silently saying, "I can slow down," could have helped her feel more centered. These simple actions send *powerful* signals of safety to her nervous system, telling the body: *You're not in danger. You're allowed to reset.* These aren't dramatic interventions, but they are effective.

DEBRIEF: What This Teaches Us

Often, what follows is not a meltdown, but a quiet unraveling—a foggy mind, a snapping tone, mounting emails, and a lingering sense that something isn't right, even if everything appears fine.

Ms. Lee didn't fail. She disconnected.

And she didn't even know it was happening.

That's what unchecked exhaustion does. It blinds you to your own depletion.

Energy check-ins are not self-indulgent. They're self-protective. They help you catch emotional drain before it spirals into reactivity, detachment, or burnout. These practices are most effective not in moments of crisis, but when everything still appears fine on the outside, even if you're starting to unravel on the inside.

Recovery doesn't always mean rest. Sometimes, it just means remembering that you matter too, not just your output, but your internal experience. The sooner you pause to notice what's happening inside, the sooner you can identify and tend to what you actually need. That's how you sustain your well-being. You don't push through. You pause long enough to listen to what your body and mind are trying to tell you.

Reconnection: Your Impact in Focus

Most teachers enter the profession with a strong sense of purpose. You want to make a difference to support students, foster growth, and contribute to something bigger than yourself. That sense of mission becomes an internal fuel. It gets you through the long days, the tough lessons, the moments when nothing goes as planned.

But over time, the weight of the educational system begins to wear that purpose down. Constant pressures, shifting policies, and a growing list of responsibilities take their toll.

You are asked to do more with less. You are measured by metrics that often don't reflect the heart of your work. You're pulled into paperwork, compliance, scheduling conflicts, data meetings, and behavioral interventions. These are tasks that often have little room for curiosity, creativity, or joy.

Each added responsibility chips away at your ability to see the deeper meaning in what you do. You may begin to feel like you are spinning your wheels, caught in a system that keeps asking without giving back.

Eventually, you may stop feeling the impact of your work altogether.

Not because the impact is minimal or missing.

But because your nervous system has become too overwhelmed to process it.

When you're in survival mode, your brain narrows its focus. You stop registering the subtle glances from your students, the ones that show they're listening, trusting, and growing. Instead, you notice the disruptions, the failures, the moments where you fall short. Over time, this can shift your internal narrative from "I'm doing meaningful work" to "Nothing I do makes a difference."

Disconnection and emotional numbness don't begin with apathy. They begin with emotional overload. You may still care. You may still show up. But something feels missing. Your "spark" dims. Your joy dulls. Your meaning, muted. You keep moving through your routines, but inside, your motivation becomes harder to sustain. You start to question what once felt clear: Why did I choose to be an educator? And can I keep going?

The first step toward healing is reconnection. It doesn't begin by fixing everything or by making the system fair or the job less demanding overnight. It begins by reclaiming your *why*–the meaning that brought you to this work. This doesn't mean pretending everything is fine. It means seeking out the moments that remind you why your presence still matters, whether it's a conversation that sticks with you, a student who opens up, or a lesson that finally clicks.

Reconnection is a practice. It's the choice to notice what is good and real, even on hard days. It's the habit of anchoring yourself to what you value, so you do not lose yourself in what the system demands. When you pause to reconnect with your purpose, you are not denying the weight of your work. You are remembering why you still carry it.

The Benefits of Reconnection: Cognitive + Neurological Insight

Earlier sections in this toolkit described how chronic stress, over-commitment, and emotional exhaustion disrupt your nervous system and diminish your ability to think clearly, rest deeply, and feel like yourself. One of the most effective ways to reverse those effects is to reconnect with your purpose, your impact, and the reasons you were first drawn to this work.

Your brain is biologically wired to seek meaning. The neurotransmitter dopamine, which fuels motivation and reward, is not only activated by accomplishments. It is also released when your actions align with your internal values (Ryan & Deci, 2000). When you support a student through a hard moment or witness growth in your classroom, your nervous system registers those experiences as valuable. These moments trigger dopamine release and reinforce a sense of purpose (Lewis, 2021).

This is not just a feeling. It is a chemical feedback loop. The brain repeats what it associates with meaning. That's one reason teaching can feel so energizing at its best. Your effort is directly tied to work that has meaning and impact.

But when pressure builds and your attention becomes fragmented, whether by constant availability, overfunctioning, or blurred boundaries, your nervous system begins to shift. The brain's reward pathways start to disengage (Ryan & Deci, 2000). Without the reinforcing power of dopamine, your motivation flattens. You might still perform the tasks of your role, but it may begin to feel like you are just going through the motions (Bromberg-Martin et al., 2010).

This loss of drive is known as amotivation, a neurological and emotional condition in which the ability to initiate purposeful action becomes impaired. It is not laziness. It is the result of prolonged disconnection from what gives your work meaning.

Fortunately, the brain can recover from this state. Research shows that even brief moments of reflection on meaningful impact can restore both emotional clarity and neurological balance. When you pause to recall a time you made a difference or reconnect with a core value, you re-engage your prefrontal cortex. This region governs long-term thinking, decision-making, and your sense of self (Ryan & Deci, 2000).

This act of reconnection signals safety to your nervous system. The signal tells your brain and body that you are not just reacting to pressure. You are participating in something meaningful. he stress from your workload and daily challenges may still be present, but your orientation toward it begins to change. You feel more centered, and the day begins to feel more navigable.

Purpose is not an extra benefit. It is a neurological necessity. Purpose restores the sense of direction that chronic stress tends to erase. And in a profession marked by constant demands and frequent overwhelm, reconnecting to your deeper "why" is an extremely sustainable practice.

The Educator Burnout Recovery Toolkit

REFLECT:

- Think of one moment when a student needed more than content.
- What did they need? How did you respond?
- What does that say about the teacher you are?

TRY THIS:

- Create a visible why: Write your teaching purpose on a sticky note and place it where you see it every morning.
- Keep an "impact log": Once a week, write down one thing that made a difference, no matter how small.
- Celebrate micro-moments: Share a meaningful exchange with a colleague during lunch or dismissal.
- Post a gratitude wall: In your classroom or office, start a wall where students or staff can post appreciation.
- Revive a passion project: Reintroduce one part of teaching you loved, be it creative writing, music, inquiry, or mentorship.

The Educator Burnout Recovery Toolkit

CASE SCENARIO:
"Mr. Salazar Forgot He Was Making a Difference"

Mr. Salazar had always been the kind of teacher who students came back to visit. He remembered birthdays, showed up at games, and found creative ways to make grammar engaging. He believed in the power of relationships, and for the first few years, that belief was enough to sustain him.

But this year felt different.

The professional demands had multiplied: lesson planning, behavior management, data entry, family communication, emotional support, and constant responsiveness, leaving little time to recover or reflect. His caseload of students with IEPs had doubled, and he was now expected to lead a district-wide literacy initiative in addition to his regular teaching load. He stayed late for meetings, skipped lunch to catch up on emails, and rarely finished his lesson plans without interruption.

Lately, he found himself walking into his classroom feeling hollow. He couldn't remember the last time he laughed with his students. When his students shared small wins—"I finally got it!"—he smiled, but there was no real joy behind it. He still did the job each day, but it felt mechanical, as if he were performing a version of the teacher he used to be.

One morning, a student named Jordan lingered after class. "Mr. Salazar," he said quietly, "I just wanted to say thanks. You're the only reason I still come to school."

Mr. Salazar nodded, muttered "You're welcome," and rushed off to a planning meeting. It wasn't until that evening, standing in his kitchen reheating leftovers, that the moment hit him. He sat down, replayed the moment in his head, and began to cry.

He hadn't even noticed that his student was struggling or that he'd made a difference in their life. His nervous system was too overloaded to register it. His heart was in the work, but his body had stopped feeling the joy, the purpose, and the presence that used to come with it.

WHAT HAPPENED: The Science in Action

Mr. Salazar was facing what some call "meaning fatigue." His work still had purpose, but he couldn't access the sense of meaning that used to drive him. Under chronic stress, the brain's reward system becomes desensitized to the effects of stress. The dopamine loop, which normally lights up when actions feel purposeful, had been dulled by overexertion, pressure, and emotional depletion.

Even though he was doing deeply impactful work, his prefrontal cortex, which is responsible for reflection, long-term thinking, and value-based decision-making, was being overridden by his limbic system, which prioritizes survival under stress. He was in a state of emotional disconnection: going through the motions without feeling connected to them.

Jordan's comment should have sparked a powerful emotional response in the moment. However, Mr. Salazar's system was so overstimulated, it took time and stillness for the weight of the moment to register.

HOW RECONNECTION COULD HAVE HELPED

Had Mr. Salazar taken even brief moments to notice how his work was helping students grow, his nervous system might have stayed more connected to the emotional rewards of teaching.

A one-minute pause at the end of class to jot down a win, a hallway moment of gratitude, or a short note to himself about something meaningful that happened could have re-engaged his reward circuitry.

These moments do not erase exhaustion, but they anchor the mind in purpose. They signal the brain that the effort of teaching holds meaning, which reactivates the dopamine system and strengthens internal motivation. They enable the prefrontal cortex to remain active, allowing teachers to think long-term and respond from a place of grounded commitment, rather than merely reacting out of survival.

DEBRIEF: What This Teaches Us

Mr. Salazar didn't stop caring about his students. He still showed up and still wanted the best for them. But he no longer felt connected to that care. The purpose that once motivated him felt out of reach. That disconnection matters because when you care but can't feel it, burnout builds quietly. And that kind of burnout is harder to recognize and even harder to recover from.

Emotional disconnection is one of the quietest signs of burnout. It doesn't always come with tears or breakdowns. Sometimes it manifests as the absence of joy, the loss of spark, or the numbness that creeps in when you're constantly doing but no longer remember why.

Reconnection isn't about sentimentality. It's about sustainability. When you pause to notice your impact, not just through test scores or data, but through growth, trust, and human connection, your brain begins to shift. It starts releasing the chemicals that motivate, restore, and reinforce why your work matters.

Mr. Salazar didn't need a new job. He needed space to remember his purpose. And once he did, the emotion returned. The spark came back. Because beneath the exhaustion, the meaning was still there, waiting to be felt.

From Survival to Renewal: Restoring Meaning and Joy in Your Work

There comes a point in teaching when what once lit you up starts to feel distant. You go through the motions. You meet expectations. You deliver lessons. Yet something feels off. The spark—the excitement of student growth, the small wins, the laughter, the creativity—starts to fade. What was once fulfilling begins to feel mechanical. You are still doing your job, but the joy that once sustained you is harder to access.

At first, this may feel like a slump, something temporary. But eventually, the numbness and disconnection start to feel permanent. You start counting the hours. You feel drained, even on days that go smoothly. The parts of the job you used to love no longer bring the same anticipation. Your focus shifts from being present to simply getting through the tasks. You may still care deeply about your students, yet the emotional connection to your work begins to fade. This disconnection is not a result of laziness or a lack of gratitude. It is emotional depletion, and it deserves your attention.

Joy is not a luxury in teaching. It is fuel. Joy powers creativity, compassion, and resilience. When it fades, your capacity to stay engaged begins to erode. A sense of compliance takes over. You begin focusing more on completing tasks than on the meaning behind them. You check the boxes. You manage the behaviors. Joy, which once energized you, becomes something you try to recall rather than something you consistently feel.

Losing joy does not mean you are failing; it simply means you are human. It is a sign that your nervous system has been operating in overdrive for too long, meeting constant demands without time to recover. Eventually, your mind shifts from curiosity to a state of survival. That shift dulls your ability to access play, creativity, humor, and the lightness that makes teaching sustainable.

This loss of joy is not the end. It is a signal that something important is missing, not just from your schedule, but from your experience of being fully present in your own classroom. Like any message from the body or brain, you can recognize and respond to it. Joy can return. It does not come back through adding more to your plate or setting bigger goals. It returns through small, intentional shifts that reconnect you with what once made the work feel meaningful.

The first step to rebuilding joy is remembering what used to bring it. Was it playing music in the classroom? Was it a unit that sparked deep student conversation? Was it trying something new, sharing laughter with your colleagues, or witnessing a student's "aha" moment? Reintroducing those moments is not a distraction from the work. It is a way to reconnect with the parts of the job that allow you to thrive rather than simply endure.

The Science of Joy: Cognitive + Neurological Insight

In the previous section, we explored how reconnecting to purpose helps restore motivation and balance your nervous system. But purpose alone is not enough. To move from survival into renewal, your nervous system also needs moments of joy, experiences that positively engage not just your mind, but your whole emotional system.

Joy is more than a fleeting emotion. It is a biological signal that your brain is experiencing alignment, connection, or growth. When joy is present, your brain releases dopamine in regions of the brain linked to motivation, focus, and memory (Lewis, 2021). At the same time, it releases oxytocin, a hormone that fosters trust, connection, and emotional bonding (Olff et al., 2013). These neurochemicals are essential, not just for your well-being, but also for creativity, learning, and resilience in the classroom.

However, when your nervous system stays in a prolonged state of stress, the brain shifts into a survival posture. As described in earlier sections, the amygdala becomes overactive, constantly scanning for threats. Meanwhile, the prefrontal cortex, the center of empathy, creativity, and thoughtful decision-making, becomes harder to access (Arnsten, 2009; Fox et al., 2015; Imad, 2022). In this state of chronic stress, it becomes difficult to experience novelty, humor, or emotional connection. You do not lose joy because you stopped caring. You lose it because your brain has been preoccupied with protecting you.

The capacity for joy returns when your nervous system experiences safety. And that safety can be cultivated through small, intentional practices. You do not need to overhaul your classroom or redesign your entire daily routine. Playing music while setting up for the day, inviting student voice into a lesson, laughing with a colleague, or adding a moment of movement or art—these are simple, sensory-rich experiences that begin to reawaken the brain's reward systems (Bentley et al., 2023). These activities engage the parasympathetic nervous system, which supports rest and recovery, lowers cortisol, and restores your emotional flexibility, the ability to adapt your feelings and responses in the moment.

These moments of joy do more than make the day feel lighter. They give your brain the signal that you are no longer in threat mode. They reconnect you to energy, to meaning, and to the relationships that make this work matter. When joy returns to your work, even in small doses, your outlook begins to shift. You notice wins more easily. You see more of the good moments with your students, and your classroom feels less like a to-do list and more like a place where people connect and learn together.

Joy is not a luxury. It is a neurological necessity. It fuels your ability to think clearly, teach creatively, and stay emotionally steady. Joy restores the connection between your values and your work, and it makes space for curiosity, humor, and care to exist, even on difficult days (Ryan & Deci, 2000; Lewis, 2021; Fekete & Deichert, 2022).

When you learn to notice, protect, and cultivate joy, you give your nervous system what it needs to sustain you, not just with endurance but with presence and heart.

TRY THIS:

- **Bring music back:** Play a classroom song that lifts your energy while students work.
- **Say yes to silliness:** Let students vote on a class mascot or dress-up day.
- **Teach one thing your way:** Break the mold for a lesson and run it like a podcast, a gallery walk, or an improv sketch.
- **Reclaim something small:** Add one decorative or personal object to your space that makes you smile.
- **Connect joy to curriculum:** Ask students how they want to show their learning, then try one of their ideas.

CASE SCENARIO:
"Ms. Nguyen Realized She Couldn't Feel It Anymore"

Ms. Nguyen had always been the teacher who brought joy into the room. She would start her mornings with music playing softly, greet every student at the door with a smile, and keep a stash of funny sticky notes that she would randomly place on students' desks. She believed in creating a classroom that felt alive.

This year, that energy was gone.

It wasn't one thing. It was everything. There are more meetings, more behavior referrals, and more data to enter. The lesson planning that used to excite her now felt like a chore. She delivered instruction the same way, hit all her marks, and kept everything under control, but something inside her felt flat.

One Thursday afternoon, after what should have been a good day, a colleague stopped by her room and said, "You've been quiet lately. Everything okay?"

Ms. Nguyen paused. She didn't know how to answer. Nothing was wrong. And yet, everything felt wrong. She was tired in a way that sleep couldn't fix. She hadn't laughed in class in weeks. She hadn't tried something new in longer than that. She realized she couldn't remember the last time teaching felt good.

That night, she sat on the edge of her bed and admitted it out loud for the first time: I think I lost the joy.

WHAT HAPPENED: The Science in Action

Ms. Nguyen was emotionally depleted. She felt a deep mental and physical fatigue caused by sustained stress, constant demands, and the absence of meaningful recovery. When you continually give without taking the time or space to restore yourself, your body stays stuck in survival mode. Over time, it dulls your capacity for joy and connection. The brain stops seeking curiosity and creativity and instead clings to predictability and control.

Although Ms. Nguyen still cared about her students and fulfilled her responsibilities, her brain had deprioritized the functions that made teaching feel joyful. Her prefrontal cortex, which regulates emotion, connection, and long-term motivation, had become harder to access. The amygdala, which detects and responds to stress and perceived threats, had become more dominant. This made change, creativity, and spontaneity feel burdensome, and joy felt distant, even when the classroom was technically calm.

She didn't stop being a good teacher. However, her experience in the classroom had become muted and mechanical.

HOW JOY COULD HAVE BEEN REKINDLED

Ms. Nguyen didn't need a major overhaul to feel joy again. What she needed was space to reconnect with the parts of teaching that once made her feel energized and alive.

That reconnection could have started with one small act of choice, such as playing a song she loved during class transitions, sharing a favorite poem, or allowing herself to laugh with her students without rushing to the next item on the agenda. Even five minutes of low-pressure creativity or a single moment of emotional connection can re-engage the brain's reward system.

Those sparks do not fix everything, but they interrupt flatness. They offer evidence to the nervous system that safety and meaning still exist. They shift the brain out of shutdown and make it easier to focus, connect, and respond with care.

DEBRIEF: What This Teaches Us

Ms. Nguyen didn't lose her love for teaching. She lost access to it. That distinction matters.

Joy fades when pressure becomes constant and recovery becomes rare. In education, it's easy to fall into a nonstop cycle of action and reaction, with little time to reflect or feel a sense of progress. The

problem is not a lack of care or effort. It is the scarcity of conditions that makes joy possible.

Reintroducing joy is not about being cheerful all the time. It is about making space to feel alive in the work again. It's about choosing moments of creativity, connection, and lightness, not because they are extra, but because they are necessary.

When teachers lose joy, it is not a sign of failure. It is a signal that their systems are asking for something more sustainable. And when they respond to that signal with care, small shifts can create real healing.

Joy can return, maybe not all at once, but through small, intentional moments. Each return is a sign that your heart is still in it. That spark is still there, and it's worth protecting.

When You're Holding the Team Together

You may be the one others count on: the steady presence during a crisis, the voice of reason in staff meetings. You check in when someone is struggling. You stay steady when others fall apart. You keep things moving. You calm the room. You solve problems before they escalate. People trust you. They lean on you. And they often assume you're fine, because you *seem* fine.

Being the reliable one carries weight. When you are the person who holds the team together, you often carry more than your share of the emotional load. You continue to be there for everyone else, even when you're running on empty. You absorb tension so others can breathe. You offer encouragement while suppressing your own doubt. You try to hold the line, but inside, you are stretched to the limit.

This quiet burden rarely comes with recognition. People may notice your strength but overlook your strain. They may not see the cost of being the person who never falls apart. Over time, you begin to believe your value lies in appearing strong for others. That belief becomes a survival mode that is difficult to leave behind.

You may stop asking for help because you fear being a burden. You may struggle to name your own needs because you are so focused on meeting everyone else's. You might downplay your stress, minimize your feelings, or talk yourself out of rest. You become the anchor, but lose touch with what keeps you grounded.

This is how burnout hides in plain sight. You may not feel like you're falling apart, but you start to feel weighed down. Numb. Quietly overwhelmed. You might carry resentment you cannot voice or exhaustion that lingers, even after rest. You may wonder why your care feels like a weight instead of a gift.

The truth is that being the emotional anchor is meaningful, but it is not sustainable without support. You cannot help others regulate if you are constantly dysregulated. You cannot model care if you are disconnected from your own needs. You cannot keep being the glue without slowly coming undone.

Restoring balance does not mean stepping away from your team; it means taking a step back. It means letting yourself be human within it. It means creating space for mutual care and support. It means building relationships where support flows both ways. And it means permitting yourself to be cared for, not just the one doing the caring.

The Cost of Being the Strong One: Cognitive + Neurological Insight

In the previous section, we explored how joy restores energy, clarity, and emotional resilience. But joy is difficult to access when you are always the one holding others up. When you are the person everyone turns to for stability, encouragement, or calm, you end up shouldering more than your share of emotional weight. Over time, that weight creates real strain on your nervous system.

This strain is not just ordinary fatigue. It is a form of chronic stress called compassion fatigue, a condition in which constant caregiving begins to deplete the systems that regulate your emotions and protect your well-being (Compassion Fatigue: Symptoms to Look For, 2024). The result is a brain that remains alert to others' needs, but disconnected from your own.

The amygdala, which monitors your environment for signs of stress or distress, becomes hyperactive. It keeps you focused on managing the needs of your team or your students. At the same time, your prefrontal cortex, the region responsible for boundary-setting, thoughtful decision-making, and emotional regulation, becomes harder to access. This imbalance between your stress-response system and your reasoning center leaves you feeling constantly on edge. You are calm on the outside, but internally bracing for the next demand.

When this high-alert state continues without relief, your autonomic nervous system also becomes dysregulated. The sympathetic branch, which drives alertness and action, remains dominant for too long. Meanwhile, the parasympathetic system—responsible for rest, recovery, and emotional reset—has fewer opportunities to engage. Without regular activation of this recovery response, your system begins to break down. You may feel exhausted, irritable, or numb. Joy becomes harder to access. Emotional flexibility diminishes.

This strain is intensified by a lack of reciprocity from colleagues, students, or even your school system. When care consistently flows in one direction, empathy begins to feel like a burden instead of a strength. The brain's mirror neuron system, which helps you attune to others, becomes overstimulated. Without moments of mutual support, even your capacity to care begins to feel like a drain.

To restore balance, your nervous system needs to feel safe receiving support, not just giving it. This begins with relational experiences that affirm your needs as valid and worthy of care (Olff et al., 2013). It could be as simple as someone checking on you without being asked, listening without interruption, or responding with compassion when you express vulnerability. Moments of genuine care release oxytocin, the hormone that signals connection and helps regulate your heart rate, stress levels, and mood.

These acts of care also rebuild emotional resilience. They remind your nervous system that connection does not require overextension. They help you internalize a new truth: you are not meant to shoulder every burden by yourself.

Leadership and caregiving do not have to come at the cost of your well-being. You can be steady and still need support. You can care deeply and still need to rest. You are not more effective when you ignore your needs. You are more effective in the long run when you tend to them.

Support is not a luxury. It is a biological necessity. Support restores the systems that keep you grounded and steady, and it creates space for joy, clarity, and presence to return.

Allowing yourself to receive care is not a weakness. It is a form of strength. It is the choice to continue this work without abandoning yourself in the process.

TRY THIS:

- **Name your role:** Write down what you've taken on emotionally at work. Then ask, "Who supports me?"
- **Set a micro-boundary:** The next time someone leans on you, pause before you say yes.
- **Create a vent-safe zone:** Set a timer with a trusted colleague for 5 minutes of uncensored venting followed by 5 minutes of shared problem-solving.
- **Trade encouragement:** Text a colleague an authentic compliment, and ask for one in return.
- **Ask for something:** Practice requesting help, coverage, or feedback, even in small ways.

CASE SCENARIO:
"Coach Bell Didn't Think Anyone Noticed"

Coach Bell was the one everyone depended on. When a fight broke out in the hallway, he was the first call to help sort things out. When the principal needed someone to cover a class, he stepped in without complaint. He stayed late to mentor students. He kept extra snacks in his office for students and staff. He organized the staff birthday list. Whenever someone on campus needed a steady hand, the first person who came to mind was Coach Bell.

Coach Bell liked being that person. He took pride in it. He had always believed in being there for others. But lately, the weight was starting to settle in his shoulders. He didn't talk about it. He didn't want to make it about him. So he just kept moving.

Then one afternoon, as he was leaving campus, he saw his own reflection in the staff entrance door. He looked tired. Not just end-of-the-day tired, but something deeper. It had been weeks since he had done anything for himself. His lunch breaks were spent handling behavior referrals. His evenings were filled with text messages from students in crisis. His weekends disappeared into planning.

No one had asked how he was doing, and he had stopped asking himself.

WHAT HAPPENED: The Science in Action

Coach Bell was showing signs of compassion fatigue. As the steady presence for his team, he became their emotional anchor. But that role exposed him to constant low-level stress without reciprocal relief. His amygdala was constantly engaged, scanning for others' emotional needs so he could respond right away. This constant alertness limited blood flow to his prefrontal cortex, making it harder for Coach Bell to reflect, keep perspective, and set personal boundaries.

These are hallmarks of a dynamic that is out of balance, where support flows out but never returns. This kept his sympathetic nervous system on high alert. He was constantly vigilant, always caring for others while bracing for something to go wrong.

The cost of caring for others at his own expense was subtle but cumulative. Emotional numbness set in. Fatigue clawed at his body. The joy he once felt in the work began to fade.

Over time, his mirror neuron system, responsible for emotional attunement and empathy, became overstimulated. He could feel the weight of everyone else's struggles, but he had no place to release his own. That kind of imbalance drained his emotional flexibility and capacity to connect with others.

HOW REGULATION COULD HAVE HELPED

Coach Bell didn't need to stop being the steady one. However, he needed time and care to steady himself first.

That shift could have started small: ten minutes to check in with a trusted colleague, a brief walk around the building with no agenda, or even saying out loud, just once, "Today was hard." Each of these moments would have signaled something vital to his nervous system: I am allowed to be cared for, too.

When someone offers you a calm, supportive presence without judgment, it sends a powerful message to your body: you're safe now. That's not just emotional support; It's a biological reset. That support activates your parasympathetic nervous system, quiets the stress response, and opens the door to renewal. Mutual care, a necessity in the teaching profession, produces oxytocin, the hormone that helps restore balance, replenish empathy, and reconnect you to the present without running yourself dry.

DEBRIEF: What This Teaches Us

Being dependable is a gift. However, when dependability becomes a disguise for exhaustion, it starts to hurt you. You are not meant to carry the emotional weight of a whole team without rest, care, or recognition.

Coach Bell did not need to stop helping others. He needed to stop doing it alone. Mutual care is not extra. It is essential. Without it, strong people break quietly.

If you are the one who holds everyone together, remember this: you are allowed to be supported too. Letting others support you is not a failure of strength. It is the practice of sustainability. And it is how you protect the very qualities that make you someone others trust.

When Boundaries Feel Impossible

You became a teacher to make a difference, to be someone students could count on. You entered this work with an open and full heart, ready to support, care, and lead. Somewhere along the way, your dedication turned into overextension.

Now, you're saying yes to one more meeting, one more student crisis, one more request for help, even with your plate already overflowing. You stay late to finish what others won't. You give up your planning period because someone else needs coverage. You answer messages at night, even though you promised yourself you wouldn't.

At first, this feels like commitment. But slowly, the line between dedication and self-abandonment starts to blur. You feel more irritable, more tired. You find yourself less present, more resentful, but unsure where to direct that feeling. After all, *you* were the one who agreed. *You* stayed. *You* didn't say no.

You may tell yourself that the feeling you're experiencing is just a season and that things will settle down soon. Once the pressure lets up, you'll take better care of yourself. However, seasons stretch into semesters. Semesters turn into years. And somewhere along the way, the habit of ignoring your own limits becomes so normalized, you forget what boundaries even look like.

This isn't just about being busy. It's about functioning from a place of depletion. You're saying yes while your nervous system screams for rest. You're doing your job while silently hoping someone will notice how much it's costing you. You're trying to be enough for everyone, while slowly disappearing from yourself.

Saying no feels selfish. Setting limits feels like letting someone down. Asking for space feels like breaking an unspoken rule. But here's the truth: you can't give what you no longer have. When your boundaries disappear, your ability to sustain empathy, clarity, and connection disappears with them. You stop thriving and start surviving, just trying to make it to the next break.

It may feel impossible to change. The culture of overwork in education is real, so is the guilt, and the fear of being perceived as difficult or uncaring. But know this: so is the cost of continuing without boundaries. That cost is your well-being. It is your presence. It is your peace. No job, no role, and no level of commitment is worth losing those parts of yourself.

Reclaiming boundaries does not mean becoming rigid or disengaged; it means setting clear limits and maintaining them. It means honoring your capacity and trusting that you matter, too. It also means staying connected to your values without sacrificing your health to meet others' expectations.

How Setting Boundaries Heals Your Nervous System: Cognitive + Neurological Insight

In earlier sections, we explored how giving support without receiving it can leave your nervous system strained. A similar process happens when you consistently ignore your limits. When your boundaries are dismissed by others or by yourself, your nervous system begins to learn that overextension is required for approval, safety, or belonging.

Each time you say yes when you mean no, or push through exhaustion to meet another demand, your nervous system encodes that pattern as necessary for survival. Over time, this creates a feedback loop. The more you override your needs, the more your body gets feedback that doing so is the only way to avoid harm or disconnection.

The amygdala, which helps your brain scan for threats, becomes increasingly sensitive to social pressure when these patterns continue over time. Saying no stops feeling like a choice. It begins to feel like a risk. You may intellectually know that you have a right to protect your time and energy, but your body responds as if setting limits is unsafe.

As this pattern repeats, your sympathetic nervous system, the system responsible for activating your stress response, stays on high alert. You may find yourself constantly anticipating disappointment, tension, or unspoken expectations, even in objectively calm moments. This kind of hypervigilance keeps your body braced and your energy drained. It also blocks access to your parasympathetic system, which supports rest, digestion, and emotional recovery (Fox et al., 2015).

Over time, the strain begins to impair your cognitive clarity. Your prefrontal cortex, the part of the brain that supports thoughtful decision-making, impulse control, and long-term planning, becomes harder to access (Goodpaster et al., 2025). You may feel reactive or scattered. You may say yes automatically, even when your body is signaling no. You may lose touch with what you want or need, because your nervous system has learned to prioritize external expectations above internal signals.

Boundaries are more than a communication tool. They are a form of neurological repair. When you begin to set small, consistent limits—whether by turning down a request, stepping away for a moment, or simply pausing before responding—you start to teach your nervous system something new. You teach it that safety is not dependent on self-sacrifice. You teach it that rest is allowed. You teach it that your needs are not threats to connection.

These moments of boundary-setting help rebalance your nervous system. They increase your ability to tolerate short-term discomfort in service of long-term well-being. They restore the rhythm between giving and receiving, action and rest. They create a sense of internal safety that allows you to move through the day with presence rather than pressure.

Boundaries are not barriers. They are structures that protect your clarity, your compassion, and your ability to contribute meaningfully without losing yourself in the process (Fox et al., 2015). Practiced with consistency and care, boundaries become one of the most effective tools for sustaining both your work and your well-being.

TRY THIS:

- Draft your "pause" script: Practice saying: "Let me check my capacity and get back to you."
- Set a visibility boundary: Put up a sticky note, lamp, or object that signals "Do Not Disturb."
- Audit your after-hours time: Track one week of evening labor. Identify what can wait.
- Pre-write your 'no': Keep a template on hand for when you need to say 'no' with kindness and clarity.
- Choose one non-negotiable: Declare a boundary you'll hold this week (e.g., no emails after 6 p.m.).

CASE SCENARIO:
"Ms. Rivera Couldn't Say No"

At first, Ms. Rivera was the go-to person. When someone needed a last-minute sub, she stepped in. When there was trouble with a parent, she handled it. When extra students were added to her roster, she said yes without hesitation. She was known for being flexible, reliable, and always willing to lend a hand.

She didn't mind in the beginning. She took pride in being the one who could manage anything. However, as the months passed, the requests continued to come. Her planning periods disappeared. Her inbox filled with late-night messages. Her lesson planning spilled into weekends. And no one seemed to notice how much it was costing her.

The Educator Burnout Recovery Toolkit

One Friday afternoon, the assistant principal popped in to ask if she could stay for an after-school event. Ms. Rivera smiled and said yes, even though she had promised her sister she'd be home early for dinner. She stayed through the event, cleaned up afterward, and drove home in silence.

That night, she lay in bed staring at the ceiling. Her chest felt tight, and her mind kept racing. It wasn't just about the missed dinner. It was about everything: the invisible toll, the constant pressure, and the slow erosion of any space that belonged to her.

WHAT HAPPENED: The Science in Action

Ms. Rivera's nervous system had adapted to living in constant overdrive. Each time she pushed past her limits to meet another demand, her brain began to treat that behavior as normal and necessary. Over time, she stopped recognizing those moments as boundary violations. Her amygdala, tuned to detect threat, became hypersensitive to subtle social cues, especially signs of disapproval. As a result, setting even a small boundary felt risky, and her body responded with anxiety.

This constant vigilance kept her sympathetic nervous system on high alert. She was always monitoring others' moods, anticipating reactions, and bracing for disappointment. Meanwhile, her prefrontal cortex, which supports long-term planning, reflection, and emotional regulation, grew overworked and depleted. As the strain built, it became harder to recognize her own limits, protect her time, or clearly assert her needs.

She wasn't failing. She wasn't disorganized. Her brain had been trained to associate saying 'yes' with safety and saying 'no' with threat. Without an intentional reset, her nervous system would continue to override her boundaries in the name of survival.

HOW REGULATION COULD HAVE HELPED

Ms. Rivera didn't need to overhaul her schedule or cut herself off from her team. What she needed was a small, steady practice of self-permission.

That shift toward self-permission could have started with just one small change. A simple pause when a new request came in. A moment to check in with her body and ask, "Do I really have the space for this?" Even a default phrase like "Let me check and get back to you" could have interrupted the reflexive "yes" long enough to allow clarity to return.

With each small, self-honoring act, her nervous system would begin to relearn that saying no is not a dangerous thing, boundary-setting is not rejection, and caring for others doesn't have to mean abandoning herself. These subtle shifts could have helped Ms. Rivera to restore her balance and make her feel safe again in her own choices.

DEBRIEF: What This Teaches Us

Boundaries are not about being less committed; they are about being more committed. They are about staying connected to your values without losing your health in the process.

Ms. Rivera thought she was being a team player. But she had been trained by experience to believe that overextension was part of being good at her job. No one taught her how to name her needs. No one modeled what healthy limits looked like. So when exhaustion set in, she blamed herself. But she wasn't broken. She was responding to a culture that praises burnout and labels recovery as a sign of weakness.

Boundaries are how we begin to repair that culture. We do this not by building walls, but by creating the space we need to engage with energy, clarity, and compassion. You do not have to say yes to prove your worth. You already matter. You matter even when you protect your time. You matter when you choose rest. You matter when you say no.

When You Feel Like You're Failing Everyone

You try. Every single day, you try. You plan thoughtful lessons, answer messages late at night, check in on the student who seems off, attend meetings prepared, and absorb more emotional weight than most people will ever understand. You carry the needs of your students, the expectations of your administrators, the worries of families, and sometimes even the unspoken pressure to hold your team together. And yet, it never feels like enough.

Educators are often taught to internalize responsibility for everything: learning gaps, behavior, family dynamics, and district pressures. So you begin to believe that any shortcoming, no matter how systemic, is your fault.

You miss one email and feel unprofessional. A student has a rough day, and you wonder if you didn't do enough to support them. Test scores dip, and you question your effectiveness. Someone asks how you're doing, and all you can think about is everything you didn't get done. Even when you give your all, you walk away feeling like you've dropped the ball.

The Educator Burnout Recovery Toolkit

You don't feel like you're failing because you're falling short. You feel that way because your nervous system is overloaded. The truth is, you are doing far more than most people could ever see. You are leading with care, effort, and intention—even when conditions are far from ideal.

However, when stress becomes constant, your brain shifts into survival mode. It starts scanning for what's wrong instead of recognizing what's working. That dread you may feel isn't a sign that you're not doing enough. It's your body's way of saying, "This is too much."

You are not failing. In fact, you're performing under pressure with strength and heart. The disconnect is not between your effort and your outcomes. It's the gap between your reality and what your brain can process when it's overwhelmed. Your struggle doesn't mean you're failing or are incapable. It means you've been pushing yourself without enough time or support to repair.

When this happens, you start noticing your missteps more than your progress. You replay moments you wish had gone differently. You fixate on the one student you couldn't reach instead of the twenty you did. You measure yourself against unrealistic standards and wonder why you come up short of them.

Over time, this pattern corrodes your confidence. You stop celebrating wins. You stop trusting your instincts. You mistakenly interpret exhaustion as incompetence. The voice in your head grows louder and says, "You're not doing enough. You're letting people down. You're failing."

That voice is not the truth. It's a symptom of exhaustion. It's the echo of your dysregulated nervous system, pushed past its limits, no longer able to recognize success.

You don't need to push harder. You don't need to become superhuman. What you need is space to see your own impact, clearly, without the fog of constant pressure. You need support that reminds you that your work matters, even when it goes unseen. And you need permission to let go of the belief that doing your best will always feel like success. Because sometimes, even your best will feel like it wasn't enough. That does not mean you've failed. That means you're human.

You're Not Actually Failing: Cognitive + Neurological Insight

The feeling that you are failing everyone, even as you manage to hold everything together, is not a reflection of your ability. It is a reflection of a nervous system overwhelmed by unrelenting stress and unreasonable expectations. When pressure outpaces support, your body struggles to register moments of success or connection. Instead, it stays locked in a pattern of urgency and self-surveillance.

This happens because your amygdala, the brain's built-in alarm system, is designed to detect threats and keep you safe. Under chronic stress, the amygdala becomes hyperactive and begins to overreact to ordinary challenges. A delayed response from a colleague, a difficult parent interaction, or a moment of classroom chaos may all feel like signs that you are falling short. This activation triggers the release of cortisol, a hormone that plays an important role in regulating stress, sleep, digestion, and mood. But when cortisol remains elevated, it fuels a vicious cycle that magnifies your sense of failure and impairs your ability to think clearly (Godoy et al., 2018).

In this state of prolonged stress, even small mistakes or routine obstacles may feel like evidence that you are not doing enough. Meanwhile, your prefrontal cortex, the part of the brain responsible for reason, perspective, and long-term thinking, becomes harder to access (Arnsten, 2009). As a result, your ability to self-regulate and see the full picture of your situation diminishes. Even when you know you are trying your best, your nervous system is not equipped to believe it. This leads to a distorted internal narrative: that you are behind, that you are letting people down, that your effort is not enough.

Moments of success in your day-to-day work become harder to register when your nervous system is stuck in stress mode. You may support dozens of students, complete multiple tasks, and navigate several challenges in a single day, but find yourself fixating on one unresolved issue. This is not a character flaw. What you experience as failure is often your brain's stress response, not an accurate reflection of your impact.

To begin shifting this pattern, your nervous system needs practice recognizing what is working. That recognition must go deeper than surface-level reassurance. When you identify a moment that went well or acknowledge something meaningful you contributed, it activates your brain's dopamine system. The same system restores motivation and supports a sense of purpose (Decker et al., 2024). These small shifts in awareness begin to challenge the stress-induced belief that you are never doing enough.

You do not need to wait for external validation. You can begin this process by naming three ways you made a difference today, even if no one noticed. These acts of self-recognition help rewire your brain to associate effort with value (Diniz et al., 2023). Over time, your nervous system learns that success in schools is not defined by perfection, but by showing up for your students with presence, care, and consistency.

This perspective does not minimize the very real challenges of your work. It offers a clearer lens through which to view your contributions. What may feel like just getting by is often a sign of quiet strength. Your continued effort, especially under stress, is not a failure. It is proof that your nervous system has been working overtime to carry a weight that was never meant to be carried alone (Fekete et al., 2022).

That feeling of failure is not the truth. It is a signal. It is your body's way of saying that it is tired, not that it is incapable. Recognizing that difference is the first step toward restoring a more accurate and compassionate view of yourself.

TRY THIS:

- Keep a "done" list: Instead of a to-do list, list what you finished today, no matter how small.
- Write like a friend: Imagine your best teacher friend had your day. Write them a note. Then read it to yourself.
- Reflect on a recovery: Think of a time something went wrong and you handled it anyway. That's capacity.
- Celebrate invisible wins: When a student smiled, a class stayed calm, or you stayed kind, those count. No wins are too small.
- Declare enough: Say aloud at the end of the day: "I was enough for today."

CASE SCENARIO:
"Mr. Daniels at His Breaking Point"

Mr. Daniels stayed late again. He wasn't behind on work, but he couldn't shake the feeling that he was missing something. A parent had emailed him three times about their child's grade. A student had stormed out earlier in the day. Another had fallen asleep during his lesson, and even though he tried not to take it personally, the moment lingered.

That night, he sat at his desk in the empty classroom and stared at the student projects he hadn't graded yet. His eyes burned. His back ached. His thoughts spun.

He had already coached soccer after school, led a team meeting, answered emails during his lunch break, and spent part of his prep period calling a parent about behavior concerns. Still, all he could focus on were the things he hadn't done: the lessons he didn't get to, the students he hadn't reached, and the answers he didn't have.

His chest felt tight. His thoughts were loud. He asked himself, "Why can't I keep up? What if I'm not cut out for this?"

WHAT HAPPENED: The Science in Action

Mr. Daniels was experiencing a classic cognitive distortion triggered by chronic stress. His amygdala had become highly reactive, scanning his day for problems and risks rather than noticing moments of growth or connection. The amygdala is the part of the brain wired for survival and for detecting danger. It doesn't measure success or track progress. When there are no immediate physical threats, the amygdala often turns its vigilance inward, scanning for personal shortcomings, and begins to target self-worth.

Although Mr. Daniels had poured energy, care, and intention into his work, his brain filtered the day through a lens of inadequacy. He couldn't see the full picture, only the parts he believed he had failed to complete. His prefrontal cortex, responsible for reflection and accurate self-assessment, was struggling to regain control. That's what unprocessed stress does. It warps the mind's ability to judge reality.

The longer this pattern continues, the more difficult it becomes to recognize success or feel a sense of accomplishment. The brain's reward system dulls, and self-criticism becomes the default filter through which individuals view themselves. Mr. Daniels wasn't failing. However, his nervous system no longer had access to perspective. And without regulation or reflection, he remained trapped in a loop of emotional depletion and unearned blame.

HOW REGULATION COULD HAVE HELPED

If Mr. Daniels had taken a moment to pause before spiraling into self-doubt, he might have interrupted the stress feedback loop that made him feel like he was failing. Even something small, such as stepping outside for a moment of stillness or jotting down three things that went well, could have signaled safety to his nervous system and shifted him out of survival mode.

A short breathing routine or a grounding technique, like planting both feet on the floor and taking one mindful breath per racing thought, might have helped redirect his attention. From that calmer state, he could have reconnected with the care, effort, and presence he gave his students throughout the day.

Even naming the negative mental pattern by saying, "I'm focusing only on what went wrong again," brings his emotions to his awareness, validates them, and activates his prefrontal cortex, allowing Mr. Daniels to shift his focus so he can begin to restore his balance. It's neurological regulation. Naming your negative thought patterns, so you can become aware of them, stop them, and shift them, brings logic back online and helps the brain see the full picture, not just the distorted fragments that feel like failure.

DEBRIEF: What This Teaches Us

Mr. Daniels didn't need a performance improvement plan. He needed support, recovery, and a reminder that caring deeply is not the same as being in control. Teaching is a layered, emotional, and often thankless profession. You can give your best and still walk away feeling like it wasn't enough. That feeling is not failure. It is a signal that your system is overloaded and your efforts are outpacing your capacity.

When you absorb unrealistic demands as personal shortcomings, you begin to carry guilt that was never yours to hold. The message becomes "Do more" instead of "You've done a lot." But more is not always the answer. Sometimes the answer is clarity. Sometimes it's rest. And often, it is the quiet practice of remembering what you've already given.

Educators like Mr. Daniels are not failing. They are operating in a culture that equates impact with constant output and emotional validation. But in reality, effort, presence, and consistency often go unrecognized. That does not make them meaningless. It makes them quietly heroic.

The next time you feel like you're falling short, ask yourself what you would say to a colleague who did everything you just did. Then say it to yourself. Say it out loud. Say it with conviction. You are not failing. You are overextending in an under-resourced system. You are worthy of support, not shame. Any inner voice that says otherwise is not telling the truth. It is a signal that it's time to pause, reset, and return to yourself.

When You're Not Sure You Can Keep Doing This

The weight of your job doesn't always build gradually. Some days, it crashes all at once. You walk into your classroom or open your laptop, and the responsibilities hit like a wave. A deep heaviness settles in, whispering, "I can't keep doing this." That thought lingers, humming beneath the surface as you imagine walking out, silencing your phone, and leaving the job behind.

You question your career. You think about other paths, other lives, and what it might feel like not to be needed by everyone, all the time.

These thoughts aren't a sign of weakness. They are signals. They are your body's way of warning you that you're overwhelmed. It means something needs to change. When mental exits feel like the only relief, your body is asking for help.

There is danger in ignoring the signs. We're taught to push through, to smile, to say yes when we're having emotional difficulty. However, continuing at the same pace without rest isn't resilience. It's depletion.

You're not the only one who's thought about quitting or who has cried in your car after work. These thoughts don't define you. They show you're still aware of your limits. It's ok to pause. You don't need to solve everything today. You need space to breathe and think clearly again.

Why Your Body Freezes, And How to Get Out of it: Cognitive + Neurological Insight

There may come a moment when pressure on you feels so relentless that you begin to question whether you can continue working in schools—or in education at all. That feeling, though deeply emotional, also has a neurological explanation. When the nervous system becomes overloaded and neither fight nor flight feels possible, the body enters a third survival state: freeze.

The freeze response is governed by the dorsal vagal complex, a part of the vagus nerve that initiates shutdown when the brain perceives danger without an escape route. This response does not look like panic. It often looks like stillness, disconnection, or numbness. You may feel emotionally flat, detached from your surroundings, or unable to make even small decisions. You might begin imagining dramatic life changes or fantasizing about quitting teaching or leaving education altogether. These thoughts are not personal failings. They are your brain's attempt to protect you from overload.

In previous sections, we explored how chronic stress can push your nervous system into overdrive. But when that stress becomes too much to bear, your system can shut down completely. This is not a weakness. Your biology is doing its best to keep you safe.

What your body needs in this state are signals that you can feel safe again. Neuroscientists call these cues "signals of safety"—sensory inputs that communicate to your brain and body that the threat has passed and renewal can begin (Sutton, 2023). These sensory inputs might include placing a hand over your heart, taking slow, regulated breaths, stepping outside for a moment, or hearing a calm voice. Even a few words from a trusted colleague or the feel of sunlight on your face can start to shift your physiology.

These actions may seem small, but they help activate the ventral vagal branch of the parasympathetic nervous system. This is the same system that supports social engagement, mental clarity, and emotional stability. When you engage it, you begin to return to yourself—not all at once, but enough to re-access your perspective-taking and decision-making abilities.

It is important not to make major life decisions while your body is in a state of shutdown. Your prefrontal cortex, the part of your brain that supports long-term thinking, reflection, and planning, is not fully accessible. The desire to escape may feel urgent, but that urgency often reflects nervous system exhaustion, not your deeper values or long-term goals.

Feeling like you can't keep going is not proof that you are failing. It is a sign that you have reached the limits of what your nervous system can handle without repair.

The path forward begins with care. Just as earlier sections emphasized the importance of boundaries, rest, and reflection, this moment calls for gentleness and support. By offering your body small experiences of safety, you begin the slow process of re-entry. Over time, your nervous system learns that it is no longer in danger, and you regain access to the part of yourself that still knows why you began this work in the first place.

TRY THIS:

- Schedule a 'nothing' block: Block off 30 minutes this week just to breathe, nap, or stare at the ceiling.
- Reconnect with nature: Spend 5 minutes outside with no agenda. Just notice.
- Plan something to look forward to: Schedule a small treat, event, or ritual that reminds you you're still alive inside.
- Make your why visible: Post photos, quotes, or symbols of why you teach near your desk.
- Tell someone the truth: Say, "I'm struggling." Let someone support you.

CASE SCENARIO:
"Ms. Lin's Driveway Confession"

Ms. Lin left school, pulled into her driveway, turned off the ignition, and sat in silence for fifteen minutes. Her hands rested on the steering wheel, but she didn't move. The house was just steps away, but the idea of walking inside to her family and having to answer one more question, make one more decision, or pretend she had energy left was too much.

She had spent her day mediating two student conflicts, emailing a parent about missing work, and managing a classroom where half her students seemed too disengaged to care. She administered a quiz, redirected off-task behavior, remained upbeat during group work, and held back her own tears during a brief bathroom break. She had told her colleagues she was "just tired" when they asked how she was doing. That was only partly true.

What she didn't tell them was that she searched for job openings during lunch. She had Googled "careers for former teachers" twice that week. She had imagined walking into her principal's office, sliding her keys across the desk, and never looking back. That image played in her head like a reel she couldn't turn off.

WHAT HAPPENED: The Science in Action

Ms. Lin's body and brain were in a freeze state. After weeks of chronic stress, her nervous system could no longer push forward. She was not lazy or dramatic. She was overloaded.

The dorsal vagal complex, part of the vagus nerve that activates under extreme stress, had taken control. Her body was not preparing to act. It was shutting down to protect her. The numbness, silence, and urge to walk away were not irrational, per se. They were survival responses.

Her thoughts of quitting were not part of a plan. They were signals of burnout. When the nervous system cannot find relief, it creates mental exits. Her brain was asking for safety in a place that no longer felt safe.

What Ms. Lin was experiencing wasn't failure. It was a warning. When you feel like you cannot go on, that's your nervous system's way of saying the load has become too much. It is a call for rest, not judgment.

HOW REGULATION COULD HAVE HELPED

Ms. Lin might have been able to intervene sooner if she had recognized her freeze state as a biological response rather than a personal failure. Intervention could have started with one small, restorative action: stepping outside for a few minutes of sunlight, calling someone who would simply listen, or placing a hand over her heart and taking a slow, intentional breath.

Even naming the experience in the moment could have helped her interrupt the freeze response. When Ms. Lin was sitting in her car, unable to walk into her house, simply saying to herself, "I'm shutting down, not giving up," might have shifted her nervous system out of shutdown. That kind of awareness activates the prefrontal cortex, the region of the brain responsible for perspective, problem-solving, and emotional regulation. Once reengaged, it helps the brain make sense of overwhelm instead of being consumed by it.

Recovery from a freeze state does not require a full reset. It begins with consistent, low-effort habits that signal safety to the body. These small practices, breathing, grounding, and gentle connection, help rebuild a sense of capacity. Over time, they become rituals that guide teachers back to presence, back to clarity, and back to themselves.

DEBRIEF: What This Teaches Us

Ms. Lin didn't need to quit teaching to feel whole again. But she did need to stop pretending she was fine. What she was feeling was her body's way of protecting her. In education, it is easy to mistake breakdowns for a sign of weakness. But breakdowns are information. They show us where something needs to change. They reveal the cost of pushing through without rest.

The most dangerous part of the freeze state is the isolation. It convinces us we are the only ones who have ever felt this way. But many educators have sat in their cars, hands on the wheel, questioning whether they could keep going. And many of those same educators have still walked back inside, not because they had to, but because they found one reason that reminded them they still mattered.

The next time you feel the urge to walk away, pause. Don't judge the feeling. Instead, listen to it. Ask what your body is trying to tell you. Then respond with care.

You are not broken. You are exhausted. And that is a truth worth honoring.

What to Do Next

Burnout recovery happens one check-in, one shift, one honest boundary at a time. Let this toolkit mark your turning point.

Try This: Return to one section tomorrow. Use it weekly. Share it with a colleague who might need it.

Want to Go Deeper?

This toolkit is just the beginning. If you're interested in 1:1 coaching, school wellness intensives, or culture reset initiatives:

Visit www.myteacherwellness.com

Email hello@myteacherwellness.com

Book a free consultation and get personalized wellness support from people who understand the weight you're carrying. https://myteacherwellness.com/20-minute-free-consultation/

References and Further Reading

Arnsten, A. F. T. (2009). Stress signalling pathways that impair prefrontal cortex structure and function. Nature Reviews Neuroscience, 10(6), 410–422. https://doi.org/10.1038/nrn2648

Bentley, T. G. K., D'Andrea-Penna, G., Rakic, M., Arce, N., LaFaille, M., Berman, R., Cooley, K., & Sprimont, P. (2023). Breathing practices for stress and anxiety reduction: Conceptual framework of implementation guidelines based on a systematic review of the published literature. Brain Sciences, 13(12), 1612. https://doi.org/10.3390/brainsci13121612

Brown, S. (2009). Play: How it shapes the brain, opens the imagination, and invigorates the soul. Avery.

Compassion fatigue: symptoms to look for. (2024, October 12). WebMD. https://www.webmd.com/mental-health/signs-compassion-fatigue

Diniz, G., Korkes, L., Tristão, L. S., Pelegrini, R., Bellodi, P. L., & Bernardo, W. M. (2023). The effects of gratitude interventions: a systematic review and meta-analysis. Einstein (São Paulo), 21. https://doi.org/10.31744/einstein_journal/2023rw0371

Fekete, E. M., & Deichert, N. T. (2022). A brief gratitude writing intervention decreased stress and negative affect during the COVID-19 pandemic. Journal of Happiness Studies, 23(6), 2427–2448. https://doi.org/10.1007/s10902-021-00472-8

Fox, A. S., Oler, J. A., Tromp, D. P., Fudge, J. L., & Kalin, N. H. (2015). Extending the amygdala in theories of threat processing. Trends in Neurosciences, 38(5), 319–329. https://doi.org/10.1016/j.tins.2015.03.002

Girotti, M., Adler, S. M., Bulin, S. E., Fucich, E. A., Paredes, D., & Morilak, D. A. (2017). Prefrontal cortex executive processes affected by chronic stress are associated with altered glutamatergic gene expression and function. *The Journal of Neuroscience, 37*(29), 6642–6651. https://doi.org/10.1523/JNEUROSCI.4009-16.2017

Goodpaster, C. M., Christensen, C. R., Alturki, M., & DeNardo, L. A. (in press). Prefrontal cortex development and its implications in mental illness. Neuropsychopharmacology.

Grounding strategies to calm your nervous system. (n.d.). Counseling & Psych Services (CAPS). https://caps.arizona.edu/grounding

Hochschild, A. R. (1983). The managed heart: Commercialization of human feeling. University of California Press.

Holland, K. (2025, April 18). Amygdala hijack: When emotion takes over. Healthline. https://www.healthline.com/health/stress/amygdala-hijack

Imad, M. (2022, January 20). *The neuroscience of toxic stress and how it shapes our teaching.* Center for Teaching Excellence and Innovation, Johns Hopkins University. https://ctei.jhu.edu/blog/neuroscience-of-toxic-stress

Jones, S., Tinubu Ali, T., & Southern Education Foundation. (2021). The high cost of low social and emotional development [Policy brief]. https://files.eric.ed.gov/fulltext/ED616255.pdf

Lewis, R. G., Florio, E., Punzo, D., & Borrelli, E. (2021). The brain's reward system in health and disease. In Advances in experimental medicine and biology (Vol. 1344, pp. 57–69). Springer. https://doi.org/10.1007/978-3-030-81147-1_4

Marken, S., & Agrawal, S. (2022, June 13). K-12 workers have highest burnout rate in U.S. Gallup.com. https://news.gallup.com/poll/393500/workers-highest-burnout-rate.aspx

Maslach, C., & Leiter, M. P. (2016). The truth about burnout: How organizations cause personal stress and what to do about it. Jossey-Bass.

Neff, K. D. (2011). *Self-compassion: The proven power of being kind to yourself.* William Morrow.

Olff, M., Frijling, J. L., Kubzansky, L. D., Bradley, B., Ellenbogen, M. A., Cardoso, C., Bartz, J. A., Yee, J. R., & Van Zuiden, M. (2013). The role of oxytocin in social bonding, stress regulation and mental health: An update on the moderating effects of context and interindividual differences. Psychoneuroendocrinology, 38(9), 1883–1894. https://doi.org/10.1016/j.psyneuen.2013.06.019

Porges, S. W. (2011). *The polyvagal theory: Neurophysiological foundations of emotions, attachment, communication, and self-regulation.* W. W. Norton & Company.

Reising, D. L. (2013). *The impact of stress on executive function in educators: A review of the literature* [Master's thesis, Vanderbilt

University]. Vanderbilt University Institutional Repository. https://ir.vanderbilt.edu/handle/1803/5845

Roeser, R. W., Schonert-Reichl, K. A., Jha, A., Cullen, M., Wallace, L., Wilensky, R., Oberle, E., Thomson, K., Taylor, C., & Harrison, J. (2013). Mindfulness training and reductions in teacher stress and burnout: Results from two randomized, waitlist-control field trials. *Journal of Educational Psychology, 105*(3), 787–804. https://doi.org/10.1037/a0032093

Ryan, R. M., & Deci, E. L. (2000). Self-determination theory and the facilitation of intrinsic motivation, social development, and well-being. *American Psychologist, 55*(1), 68–78. https://doi.org/10.1037/0003-066X.55.1.68

Sutton, J. (2025, April 14). 18 polyvagal theory & how to use the exercises in therapy. PositivePsychology.com. https://positivepsychology.com/polyvagal-theory/

Thayer, J. F., Åhs, F., Fredrikson, M., Sollers III, J. J., & Wager, T. D. (2012). A meta-analysis of heart rate variability and neuroimaging studies: Implications for heart rate variability as a marker of stress and health. *Neuroscience & Biobehavioral Reviews, 36*(2), 747–756. https://doi.org/10.1016/j.neubiorev.2011.11.009

Victor, T. A., Khalsa, S. S., Simmons, W. K., Feinstein, J. S., & Paulus, M. P. (2024). Stress disrupts working memory and alters executive function: A neuroimaging investigation. *Scientific Reports, 14*, Article 53819. https://doi.org/10.1038/s41598-024-53819-1

Walker, T. (2021, November 12). Getting serious about teacher burnout. NEA Today. https://www.nea.org/nea-today/all-news-articles/getting-serious-about-teacher-burnout

About the Author

Dr. Zachary Scott Robbins is an experienced educator and advocate for teacher well-being. With over two decades of leadership in public education, he has supported schools in building stronger learning environments while honoring the humanity of the educators who sustain them. Through his work with MyTeacherWellness.com and Zhazoe Press, LLC, he creates practical, research-informed resources that help teachers set boundaries, recover from burnout, and reconnect with their purpose. His writing blends neuroscience, lived experience, and a deep respect for the work of teaching.

www.zacrobbins.com

www.ingramcontent.com/pod-product-compliance
Lightning Source LLC
Chambersburg PA
CBHW070206100426
42743CB00013B/3072